The Ultimate Riddles Book

Word Riddles
Brain Teasers
Logic Puzzles
Math Problems
Trick Questions

*

J.J. Wiggins

ISBN: 978-1544911960
Edition: 1.0

"A puzzle a day keeps the doctor away."
— Unknown

Contents

Riddles

1. A Message From Aliens

While monitoring space for extraterrestrial life, scientists discover that Earth will soon be visited by aliens. They receive the following message:

The brightest minds around the word scramble to figure out what it means. Are the aliens going to attack Earth, or are they friendly?

2. On Valentine's Day

A woman gets into an accident and can't remember who she is or her family. The police ask her if there's anyone they could call. She thinks for a bit and says, "On Valentine's Day, we had pie and talked about a George Orwell book."

The police think nothing of it at first, but then one of them realizes the significance of what she said. The knowledgeable officer dials a 9-digit phone number and reaches the woman's husband.

What is the phone number?

3. John's Car

John and his wife own a car that fits a maximum of 5 people. He drives Molly to work everyday. On his way, he drops his three kids off at school, and his mom at the mall. How did everyone fit in the car?

4. Making Muffins

You're making muffins and need to add 1/3 (one third) of a cup of sugar to the batter. You check the cupboards and find that you only have the following measuring cups: a 2/3 (two thirds) cup, and a 1/2 (half) cup. The muffin recipe requires exactly 1/3 of a cup of sugar. How can you accurately add this amount to the batter?

5. The Angry Astrologist

The angry astrologist has locked you up in a series of a rooms. With your superior thinking abilities, you escape them one by one, until you reach the final room.

There's a locked door with an electronic keypad with the numbers 0 to 9, and it only takes 4 digits. In the middle of the room, there's a table with information about the zodiacs.

Aquarius	January-February
Pisces	February-March
Aries	March-April
Taurus	April-May
Gemini	May-June
Cancer	June-July
Leo	July-August
Virgo	August-September
Libra	September-October
Scorpio	October-November
Sagittarius	November-December
Capricorn	December-January

You look around for more clues and stumble across something rather interesting. Above the door are three drawings from left to right: a set of scales, two fishes swimming in a circle, and a goat.

Suddenly, the angry astrologist announces, "You have five minutes to escape. But if you enter the wrong code, you'll be in for a huge surprise! Since my favorite holiday is coming soon, I'm feeling generous, so here's a hint...just kidding! No hints! Hahahahaha!"

The angry astrologist always talks in riddles, so you're quite sure there was a hint in what she said.

Time is running out!

Can you figure out the 4-digit code?

6. Folding Shirts

Steve and Melanie have jobs folding shirts at a store. Every day, they each have 100 shirts to fold. When they finish folding, they can leave. On the first day of the job, Melanie finishes folding in one and a half hours (90 minutes) and leaves, but Steve still has 10 shirts left. The next day, Steve decides to be crafty. When Melanie's not looking, he moves 5 shirts from his pile to her pile. This means that Melanie will be folding 105 shirts, and Steve 95 shirts. Steve believes he'll finish at the same time as Melanie, but is surprised when she once again finishes before him.

Assuming that both Steve and Melanie's folding speeds never change, why was Steve wrong about his prediction?

7. Mystery Man

Can you figure out who this is?

I'm big, I'm small
I can spit fireballs
When I'm on the TV
kids want to play with me
My brother's not as popular
'cause he wears a green hat
I have a red one
I can only tell you that

8. The Three-Legged Race

At a festival, you and your friends (Jacky, Chris, Martha) are competing in a Three-Legged Race. The race starts with 2 people at a time with ankles tied together navigating a track. At the end of the track, one person must run and bring the ropes back to the beginning of the track. Then, 2 more people (one of them can be the runner) with ankles tied go through the track again. This repeats until all 4 people on the team reach the end of the track.

After weeks of practice, this is how each of your teammates perform:

Three-Legged Walking Speed	
You	4 minutes
Jacky	6 minutes
Chris	7 minutes
Martha	10 minutes
Running Speed	
You	2 minutes
Jacky	1 minute
Chris	45 seconds
Martha	30 seconds

The time it takes to walk the track is the slowest of the 2 people doing the walk. For example, you and Martha would take 10 minutes to do the walk, and Chris and Martha would also take 10 minutes.

Last year's record for the Three-Legged Race was 25 minutes. Can your team beat it?

7

9. Lily's Birthday

Lily is having a birthday party at her house in a few days. In order to be invited, people have to bring with them a gift. But it can't just be any gift, it has to be something Lily approves. Very soon, a list is going around with names of people who have been invited and what they're bringing.

PARTY GIFTS & GUEST LIST	
APPLES	AMELIA
BALLOONS	BOB
CAKE	ERIC
EGGS	JOANNE, STEVE, PETE
HOTDOGS	BETH
NOODLES	JOANATHAN, EILEEN

Sally wants to go to the birthday party. What can she bring in order to be invited?

10. Lost Time

Jack is a truck driver from Springfield, Illinois. On one of his trips to Louisville, Kentucky, something bizarre happened. He left Springfield at 8:00 PM and arrived in Louisville 4 hours later. Then he checked into a motel and slept for 8 hours. When he woke up the following day, it was already 10:00 AM. How did that happen?

11. Next Tuesday

If tomorrow is two days before Tuesday, how many days before it's Tuesday two days from today?

12. Strange Sentences

Which of the following sentences is the odd one out?

A) Matrices are too hard!
B) Maracas, ukuleles, saxophones, Irish castanets.
C) Human intentions strange; they often remember yesterday.
D) Stars, planets, asteroids, comets. Endless.
E) So, can I eat now (chewing everything)?

13. Lara's Choice

While hunting for treasure, Lara comes across an area with three tunnels (A, B, C), each with a label next to its entrance.

A) A tunnel full of cute, but very hungry, man-eating bunnies.
B) A tunnel full of poisonous gas with no cure.
C) A tunnel full of laser-shooting robots programmed to kill everything and everyone on sight.

Which tunnel should she choose?

14. A Simple Word Game

Marty wants to play a word game with his friends. He writes down a few words and tells them how much they are worth in points.

```
MATH - 1 point
TREE - 1 point
HAND - 2 points
BOMB - 5 points
WING - 0 points
FINS - 0 points
```

He gives them this clue, "Count the fields, get the points."

How many points is WORD GAME worth?

15. A Strange Party

There are 100 very strange people at a party. They will only shake hands with someone if the other person says 'hello' to them first. At the end of the party, how many people will have shaken hands with each other?

16. Three Different Jobs

Three people named Mary, Alice, and Steve all have different jobs as either a nurse, an elementary school teacher, or a police officer. If Mary is afraid of blood, and neither she nor Steve likes kids, what is Steve's job?

17. New Math

Your quirky teacher comes up with a new Math operation called "@" and wants to see if you can figure out what it does. She writes the following examples on the blackboard:

$$8@5 = 31340$$
$$9@3 = 61227$$
$$10@9 = 11990$$

What's the answer for 7@6?

18. Family Day

A family of 5 is at home doing various chores and activities around the house. The mom, Amanda, is in the kitchen preparing food. The dad, John, is in the garage repairing the car. Tracy is in the basement playing ping pong. Max is mowing the lawn in the backyard. The 5th family member is Peter. Where is he and what is he doing?

19. Milk And Eggs

Mary has a password-protected smart phone, but she's not very good at remembering numbers. She decides to come up with a simple mnemonic, "My favorite things are MILK and EGGS."

Her password is 4-digits long. What is it?

20. Two Lies And A Truth

You're babysitting three kids: Mary, Mark, and Mindy. Their parents tell you 2 of them likes lying and 1 of them only knows how to tell the truth.

You ask the kids, "Which one of you is the smartest?"
Mary says, "I'm not."
Mark says, "Mindy is."
Mindy says, "Mark is lying."

Who's telling the truth?

21. Mystery Letters

What letter comes next?

A B G D E Z E __

22. Spiders And Dead Flies

How many spiders are there in a room if in each of the eight corner there's a spider, and below or above each spider are 4 spiders, but only 3 spider webs and 2 dead flies are lying around?

23. Penguin Escape

3 zookeepers and 3 penguins arrive at a river which they must cross to get back to the zoo. There's a boat they can use, but it can only hold up to 3 of them at once. Since penguins can't row, it's up to the zookeepers to do all the work. However, there's a problem! A zookeeper must always been present to watch the penguins, and, each zookeeper can only keep an eye on 2 penguins at a time. If there are no zookeepers on a side of the river where there are one or more penguins, the penguins run off. If there are 3 penguins on one side with only 1 zookeeper present, the penguins also escape.

How can the zookeepers plan their trip across the river so that they all arrive back at the zoo with all the penguins?

24. Out Of Order

Which month comes next?

MAY, JUNE, JULY,
MARCH, APRIL, AUGUST,
JANUARY, OCTOBER, _____

25. Two Dancers

Two dancers say that Nancy is their sister, but Nancy says she doesn't have any sisters. How is that possible?

26. Cute Little Things

Can you figure out this riddle?

Grab one of these from the night sky
And flip it around
You'll get these cute little things
That make kiss-y sounds

What are these cute little things?

27. World Map

Without looking at the world map, how many countries separate Poland and North Korea?

28. Splitting Spaghetti

Amy and Adam have a pot of spaghetti they'd like to split between the two of them. After 10 minutes of arguing with each other about who's bowl has more spaghetti, their dad decides to step in and offer a suggestion.

SPAGHETTI

Without actually having to weigh the spaghetti or counting the number of noodles, can you find an easy way for the kids to split the spaghetti so that both are happy with what they get?

29. Counting Numbers

In the number sequence below, what comes next?

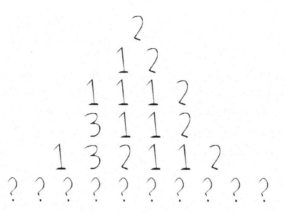

30. Three Coins

Tyler has 3 coins totaling 16 cents. One of them is not a penny or a nickel, and the other two are not dimes. What does Tyler have?

31. Thirty Apples

There are 27 apples in a basket. Four friends split it four ways, giving them 6 each, and leaving 1 in the basket. 3 more apples are then added to the basket. Then, each friend takes 1 apple.

We started with 27 apples in the basket, and 3 more makes 30 apples. How can 30 apples be split four ways?

32. Death Or Freedom

The king has sentenced you to death. On the day of your execution, he's in a good mood and decides to give you a chance to live. His servant shows you 3 cards facing down and tells you that each of them has written on them either the word DEATH or FREEDOM. At least 1 of the cards has DEATH on it, but not all 3.

The servant asks you to choose a card without looking at it, and you do so. Then, he turns over one of the other cards, and it has DEATH on it.

You are now given two options:

A) Keep your card.
B) Switch to the other face-down card.

The card you choose will be your fate. Which option should you go with?

33. Counting Heads

Mimi takes the bus to school everyday. To get through the boredom of the long commute, she likes to count the number of heads on the bus. When she first gets on, she walks pass 10 passengers and takes a seat all the way at the back. At the first stop, 3 passengers get off and 5 get on. At the next stop, 1 gets off and 2 get on. At the third stop, 8 get off and 5 get on.

At this point, she does her counting. Including Mimi, how many heads are there on the bus?

34. Playing With Percentages

Starting with a random number, you decrease that number by 50%. Then, you increase the new number by 90%. Is the final number less than, equal to, or greater than the number you started with?

35. Cash And Points

A supermarket has a special offer that gives customers 1 point and $2 cash back for every $10 they spend at the store. You have $154. How many points can you collect?

36. Twin Brothers

Nobody can tell twin brothers John and Jake apart. Not even their mother. Jake always tells the truth, but John always lies about who he is. If she asks John a simple question like "What color is the sky?", he'll answer correctly.

What question can she ask one of the twins to determine who is who?

37. A Pair Of Jeans

You pay $55 for a pair of jeans, including tax. If the pair of jeans is $50 more than the tax, how much did you pay in tax?

$ $ $

38. A Fast Foot Race

If you're in first place in a foot race and suddenly the person in third place overtakes you, what place do you fall to?

39. Sarah's Mother

Sarah's mother has three sisters: Maria, Cindy, and Carol. Each sister has a sister named Joanne. What is Sarah's mother's name?

40. Around The World

A museum in Australia has just been robbed by an art thief. At the crime scene, police find a note: "I'm making a trip around the world. Catch me if you can!" A few days later, an art exhibit in Russia reports missing paintings. Then three days later, an art collector in Oman files a report. There's seemingly no pattern to the art thief's targets. Museums in Uruguay, New Zealand, Denmark, Thailand, and Hungary become the next victims.

Agent Smarter is finally hired by international authorities to track the art thief down. He examines the clues and realizes what the thief was trying to say in her note. He knows exactly where she's heading next.

Which country will the art thief visit next?

41. Rock, Paper, Scissors

You and 32 friends are having a "Rock, Paper, Scissors" tournament. Each match, 2 people go against each other, and the winner continues to the next round.

How many matches would it take to determine the champion?

42. Three Switches

You enter a room and see a panel with 3 switches from left to right. Each switch has three positions: UP, DOWN, and NEUTRAL. All of them are currently NEUTRAL.

Beyond the room is a tunnel filled with traps. You know that in order to dismantle the traps, you have to set the switches to the correct positions.

This is the information you have:

* The number of switches in the UP position is the same as the number of switches in the DOWN position

* There are no switches to the left or right of a switch set to NEUTRAL.

What are the correct positions for the 3 switches?

43. Vowels And Consonants

Fill in the two blanks with number words so that the sentence is correct.

There are _____ vowels and _____ consonants in this sentence.

44. Hidden Animal

There's an animal hiding in the words below. What is it?

__ O R S E

B __ S O N

__ L A T Y __ U S

__ __ __ S S U M

C H E E __ __ H

E __ U

O C T O P __ __

45. Alex's Family

Alex has a mother, a father, and a brother named Scott. However, Scott does not have any brothers. How is this possible?

46. Who's Playing What

If every person who plays Minecraft also plays Pokemon Go, and some people who play Roblox play Pokemon Go, then some people who play Roblox definitely play Minecraft.

Is this statement true, false, or is there not enough information to know?

47. Five Golden Rings

In the Christmas song "The Twelve Days of Christmas," how many golden rings do you have after 12 days of Christmas?

48. Underwater

If some animals live underwater, and some other animals drink water, what do fish breathe?

49. A Thousand Lumberjacks

There are 1000 lumberjacks, and they can all chop down trees at exactly the same speed. If it takes 5 lumberjacks 5 minutes to chop down 5 trees, how many minutes does it take 1000 lumberjacks to chop down 1000 trees?

50. Simple Addition

Little Charlie added 2 to 11 and got 1 as the answer. He then added 6 to 55 and also got 1 again as the answer.

His mother gave him a cookie for answering correctly. How come?

51. Birthday Candles

It's your great great grandmother's birthday, and you are in charge of buying birthday candles for the cake. You can't quite remember how old she is, but you know she's turning at least 99 and at most 101. At the store, you see some number candles '1' to '9,' each sold separately. How many candles should you buy to ensure you get your great great grandmother's correct age?

52. Cryptic Poem

Can you decipher the poem below and figure out what two words go in the blanks?

> *An astronomer is a moon starer*
> *The statue of liberty is built to stay free*
> *To listen is to be silent*
> *The eyes, _____ _____*

53. Strange Letter Sequence

Can you find a common word that has the following sequence?

The sequence of letters can appear anywhere in the word, but must be in the order shown.

54. Impossible Age?

I have a brother named Mark. Next year, he'll be four times as old as I will be. But in three years, he'll only be twice as old as me. How old am I right now?

55. Double Money

Sally owes Tom some money. Their agreement is that whatever amount is owed by Sally at the end of a month, Tom will double it, increasing the amount she has to pay. For example, if Sally still owed Tom $10 at the end of the first month, that number would double to $20. If at the end of the second month, she still owed him $20, it would double to $40.

At the beginning of the first month, Sally pays Tom some money. At the beginning of the second month, she pays Tom the same amount of money as she did the previous month. At the beginning of the third month, she pays Tom the same amount again, and she no longer owes him any money.

Assuming the amount owed and Sally's payments are in whole dollars (no cents), at least how much did she owe Tom at the beginning, and how much did she pay him each month?

56. Big Family

Jimmy has a mom and a dad (Joanne and David), 4 grandparents (Steve, Marie, Tom, and Nancy), 1 uncle (Mark), 2 aunts (Tina and Tracy), and 3 siblings (Carl, Maggie, and Tyler). The 4 grandparents have 4 grandchildren. What are the grandchildren's names?

57. Mystery Words

Look closely. Which one of the following words does not belong in the group?

58. Zombie Virus

A zombie virus is spreading throughout the world, and there is no hope. Every day that passes, the total number of people infected doubles. If the virus takes 30 days to infect every person in the world, how many days does it take to infect half the world?

59. Kitchen Gloves

Martha has 15 pairs of kitchen gloves (15 for the left hand, 15 for the right hand) that she uses to wash dishes. The left-handed gloves wear out in 2 days, while the right-handed gloves wear out in 1 day because she uses it more often. If Martha washes dishes everyday, how many days before she has to buy more gloves?

60. It's Thanksgiving Again

Amy is a very busy person. Last month, she drove a car to visit her parents for Thanksgiving dinner. Three weeks ago, she made Halloween costumes for her sons. Two weeks ago, she saw an opera at the Metropolitan Opera in New York City. Last week, she flew to Asia for a business conference. Today, she bought a huge turkey at the supermarket and celebrated Thanksgiving with her family.

Where are Amy's parents from?

61. Blind Date

Justin's friend has set him up on a blind date with a woman named Jenny. At a small dinner party, he meets a flight attendant, a nurse, a receptionist, and a teacher. His friend never provided any pictures of Jenny, yet Justin guesses immediately that it's the teacher without even asking her name. How is he so sure?

62. Mandy's Sister

What word goes in the blank?

> *Jessica is Mandy's sister.*
> *Mandy is the _____ of Jessica's sister.*

63. Even Heart

You are shown 4 cards, 2 facing up and 2 facing down. The cards facing up has either an odd or an even number. The cards facing down has either a heart or a clubs symbol.

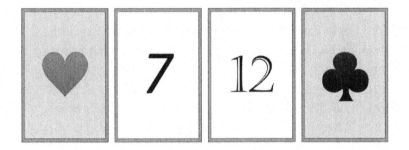

Which card(s) should you turn over to verify that the following rule is true? What cards do you not need to check?

Rule: If the number is EVEN, it must be a HEART card.

64. The Jackson Family

Mr. and Mrs. Jackson have 2 daughters, and each daughter has 1 sister and 1 brother. How many people are in the Jackson family?

65. Red Fruits

Red is Tina's favorite color. She has a bowl with three fruits in it: a watermelon, a tomato, and an apple. However, there are no red fruits in the bowl. How is this possible?

66. Body Painting

Two body painting artists have to paint 3 models for a show. Both artists paint at exactly the same speed. Each side of the body (front side and back side) takes 1 hour to paint. However, the artists don't like painting the same model at the same time. They always work on different models.

How many hours will it take them to paint the fronts and backs of all the models?

67. Strange Seating Plan

A quirky teacher decides to change the seating plan for her class of 9 kids. She doesn't tell them where to sit, but instead gives them the following instructions.

* Students with names starting with the same letter cannot side next to each other (left, right, up, or down)

* Students must sit next to at least one person of the opposite gender

The classroom has 9 seats as shown in the picture.

Seat 1	Seat 2	Seat 3
Seat 4	Seat 5	Seat 6
Seat 7	Seat 8	Seat 9

Here's the list of students.

Boys	Peter, Mark, Joseph, Andy
Girls	Francine, Cindy Patricia, Carol, April

Can you figure out an appropriate seating plan for these kids?

68. Game Show For Logicians

On a game show for people with amazing logic skills, three contestants (A, B, C) must work together to win the grand prize.

First, the contestants are placed in standing positions. The host then shows them 4 stickers: 2 smiley face stickers, and 2 sad face stickers. One by one, he puts a sticker on each person's back. The host hides the remaining sticker. The result is shown in the diagram below.

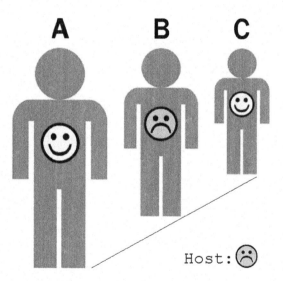

* C's back is facing the other contestants and therefore can't see any of them

* B is facing the same direction as C and can only see C's back. B can't see A at all

* A is also facing the same direction as B and C, and can see both B and C's backs

Game Show Rules:

* The contestants are not allowed to talk to each other or say anything except to guess their sticker

* The contestants are not allowed to move, turn around, make hand gestures, etc.

If any of the contestants can correctly guess the type of sticker on his back, the whole group wins the grand prize. If any of them guesses wrong, they all lose.

The host tells the them they have 60 seconds to give an answer, and the game begins.

50 seconds into the game, none of the contestants has provided an answer. Realizing that A hasn't answered, B believes he knows with a hundred percent certainty the type of sticker on his back. He gives the correct answer, and the whole group wins.

How did contestant B figure out the type of sticker on his back?

69. Two Swimmers

Two swimmers are standing next to an indoors, rectangular swimming pool. One swimmer is looking in one direction and sees a wall. The other swimmer is looking in the opposite direction and also sees a wall. However, they can both see each other and the swimming pool. How is this possible?

70. Jake's Family

A friend asks Jake about a picture of a girl on his desk. Jake tells the friend, "My mother has two children, but I have none. That girl's father, is my mother's son."

How is Jake and the girl related?

71. Seven Sevens

Your calculator is broken. The only keys working are:

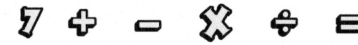

The "7" button will only work 7 times.

How can you get your calculator to show 100?

72. Escape The Tombs

Luke and Adam are treasure hunters, escaping the tombs. They reach an area with 3 tunnels (A, B, C), but can't remember which one leads to the exit, only that it is the longest of the three. The table below shows how fast each person can go down a tunnel one-way.

	Tunnel A	Tunnel B	Tunnel C
Luke	1 minute	2 minutes	5 minutes
Adam	3 minutes	6 minutes	15 minutes
Luke & Adam	2 minutes	4 minutes	10 minutes

This means that if Luke picks one tunnel and it turns out to be Tunnel A, it will take him a total of 2 minutes to get back to the main area. If Adam picks one tunnel and it turns out to be Tunnel B, it will take him a total of 12 minutes to get back to the main area. Luke can also carry Adam on his back, allowing Adam to move faster, but that slows him down.

Rules:

* They are allowed to backtrack
* They can communicate by yelling to each other if one person is in a tunnel and the other is in the main area, but not if they are in different tunnels

They have less than 16 minutes before the walls collapse. How can Luke and Adam plan it so that they both escape the tombs in time?

73. Four Heads Or Tails

4 coins are placed in a 2x2 square, some are
HEADS, and some coins are TAILS.

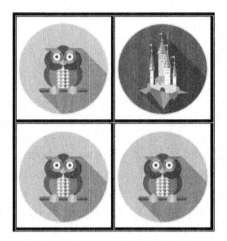

Your friend challenges you to flip them all to
HEADS or all to TAILS. You are to do this
blindfolded. Each turn goes as follows:

* You select any 1 or 2 coins to examine (you can
tell HEADS and TAILS apart)
* You may then flip over no coins, 1 coin, or 2 coins
* The square is then rotated by a random angle
* The next turn begins

Can you think of a way to flip the coins so that you
win every time without relying on luck? Remember,
you're blindfolded!

74. The Spy's Secret

Two secret agents working for competing agencies are after a spy who has been evading their every move for years. The agents have narrowed down the spy's whereabouts to a list of cities and countries.

Canada	Paris, London, Vancouver
England	Birmingham, London, Oxford
France	Lyon, Nice, Paris
USA	Paris, Vancouver

One day, they each receive an envelop from the spy. Inside Agent #1's envelop is a note with the name of a country written on it. Inside Agent #2's envelop is a note with the name of a city written on it. The agents, each wanting to be the first to catch the spy, do not reveal their clue to each other. Nevertheless, they call each other up to talk.

Agent #1: *I know which country he's in.*
Agent #2: *And I know the city.*
Agent #1: *Oh, but you'll never catch him before I do, because there's no way you can figure out the country.*
Agent #2: *Is that so? You seem quite confident. Aha, I know exactly where he is now!*
Agent #1: *You do? That means he can only be in...*

Which city and country is the spy in?

75. Cows Beneath Antarctica

What's unusual about the sentence below?

Zapping yellow xylophones with very ugly tambourines, singing rhythms quite perfectly outside, nudging many lovely kangaroos, jumping into happy giraffes, exploded deadly cows beneath Antarctica.

76. Cheese Cutting

You have a knife with 2 parallel blades that can split anything into 3 parts with a single cut. What's the most pieces of cheese you can cut from a round block of cheese if you cut it 3 times?

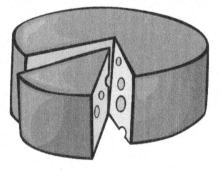

77. Wally's Weight

Wally the Wombat's weight is 50 kilograms and half his weight. What is Wally's weight?

78. Letter Pattern

Look at the letters below.

A H I M T U V W X Y

Which other letter belongs in the group?

79. Buttons On, Buttons Off

You're locked in a room with a 3x3 panel of buttons as shown in the picture.

	A	B	C
1	OFF	OFF	OFF
2	OFF	OFF	OFF
3	OFF	OFF	OFF

When a button is pressed, that button and all adjacent buttons (up, down, left, right) are affected. If a button is OFF, it will turn ON. If it's ON, it will turn OFF. For example if you pressed button A1, then buttons B1 and A2 will also be affected (and turn ON).

The buttons are currently all OFF. Your objective is to turn them all ON. Which buttons should you press?

80. The Numbers Freak

A numbers freak has locked you and 4 other people in his house. One day, he decides to give you all a chance to escape, that is, if you can solve his numbers riddle. He explains the rules. He will say a number from 1 to 5, then each person must respond with a number also from 1 to 5. If the person answers correctly, he will be allowed to leave the house. You find out that you're the last person to go.

One by one, each person plays the game, and it unfolds like so:

Numbers Freak: *1.*
Person A: *5.*
Numbers Freak: *Wrong. The correct answer is 3.*
Numbers Freak: *2.*
Person B: *3.*
Numbers Freak: *Correct. You may leave.*
Numbers Freak: *3.*
Person C: *3.*
Numbers Freak: *Wrong. The correct answer is 5.*
Numbers Freak: *4.*
Person D: *4.*
Numbers Freak: *Correct. You may leave.*

Now, it's your turn.

Numbers Freak: *5.*

What should you respond with: 1, 2, 3, 4, or 5?

81. Kitchen Counter

You own a store that sells marble kitchen counters at 8 feet by 5 feet in size. A potential customer tells you he needs a 10x4 counter.

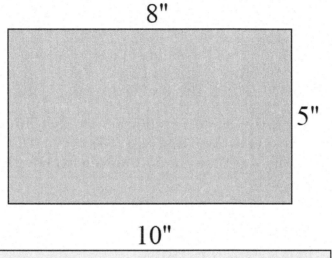

Not wanting to turn down business, you think for a moment and come up with a simple solution the customer is happy with.

How can you make just one cut to the 8x5 counter and rearrange it into a 10x4?

82. Mothers And Daughters

Three mothers and three daughters go shopping together.

Afterwards they go to a restaurant to have dinner. The hostess sees them and asks, "Table for 4?" One of them answers, "No, for 5." Can you explain the woman's answer?

83. Spies And Traitors

There are 3 people: Tom, Joseph, and Cindy. Tom is a secret agent. Cindy is a traitor. Tom is spying on Joseph, and Joseph is spying on Cindy. Is a secret agent spying on a traitor? Yes, no, or not enough information to go on?

84. Three Brothers

What word goes in the blank?

Jimmy, Tommy, and Marty are brothers. Jimmy is younger than Tommy. Marty is older than Tommy. So, Marty is _____ older than Jimmy.

85. Fast And Furious

I'm fast and furious
Behind me might be flames
Forwards, backwards
You can drive me all the same

What am I?

86. The Camping Trip

Three friends decide to do a trip at a park. Each of them brings some food and equipment.

Equipment	tent, tarp, canoe
Food	steak, eggs, potatoes

The following are details of what the friends brought to the camping trip:

* Marty brought steak
* The person with the tent brought eggs
* Josephine either owns a canoe or she brought potatoes

Which food and which camping equipment did Tamara bring on the trip?

87. Two Elevators

An office building has 2 elevators: Elevator A goes from the ground to floor 11; Elevator B goes from floor 11 to floor 21. This means that to get to the top or bottom of the building, you have to ride both elevators. Other than that, they are identical. Each can accommodate a maximum of 7 people at a time. The ride in one direction takes 30 seconds.

One strange afternoon, many of the floor buttons in the elevator buttons stop working. The only ones working are: the buttons to call the elevators to floor 21 and floor 11, the floor 11 button inside Elevator B, and the Ground Floor button in elevator A.

20 people leaving work at the same time are trying to get from floor 21 to the ground floor. Someone presses a button, and they all wait. Soon, Elevator A arrives. How should they plan the rides so that it takes the least amount of time in total for all of them to get to the ground floor?

Rules:

* You can ignore the time it takes to get off Elevator A and get on Elevator B

* Elevator A starts at floor 11, and Elevator B starts at the floor 21

44

88. They Come In Pairs

Jessica has 1 pair of socks, 1 pair of gloves, and 1 pair of jeans. How many pieces of clothing does she have?

89. Pokemon Average

Ten friends are playing Pokemon Go and have collected lots of pokemon. They want to know the average number of pokemon the group has caught and whether each of them is above or below average. None of them wants to tell each other how many they've captured.

Here's how many pokemon each person has:

Pokemon Captured	
Dan	151
Steve	223
Joe	66
Marvin	90
Anne	25
Lee	50
Chloe	133
Pete	299
Mark	165
Natalie	88

Total = 1290
Average = 1290 ÷ 10 = 129 pokemon

How can they figure out the average and still keep their number a secret?

90. The King's Revenge

You solve the Death or Freedom riddle, which infuriates the king. He does want you dead after all! Of course, he can't go back on his word or he'll lose reputation. Instead, he offers you a chance to save a friend. The two of you must play the game again, and the results will determine your fate.

Risky as it is, you decide to play, thinking your odds of winning are good.

To your horror, the king reveals a completely different game. His servant shows you 4 cards: 2 are DEATH and 2 are FREEDOM. Then, he shuffles them facing down and hands a card to you, your friend, the king, and himself. The king's card will remain a secret. You, your friend, and the servant are to hold the cards above your heads so that everyone can see each other's card except one's own card.

Rules:

* You're not allowed to speak or make hand gestures or you will be executed immediately

* You and your friend each have one turn to make a move. You can either keep your card, or trade it with another person, including the king's hidden card

* The king and his servant won't be making any moves

46

The object of the game is simple: You and your friend must finish the game with the FREEDOM card. If you finish with a DEATH card, you will be executed. If your friend finishes with a DEATH card, he will be executed.

You see that your friend has the DEATH card, and the servant has the FREEDOM card.

When the game begins, the king announces that your friend must make the first move, and you, the second move. After some consideration, your friend trades cards with the servant. He now has the FREEDOM card.

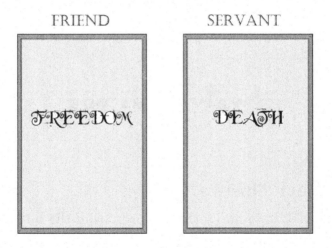

It's your turn, and you realize the king has set you up. Any other scenario would've been easy to figure out. You could always save yourself and trade with your friend, but you decide against that.

Should you keep your card or trade with the king?

91. Unmarried Men

In a family with two parents and their children, all of them except two are adults, all of them except three are married, and all of them except four are female. Alice is the youngest child and Cindy is the oldest. Are there definitely at least one unmarried adult man in the family, regardless of how big it is?

92. Word Math

Look carefully. What is interesting about the following statement?

$$eleven\ plus\ two$$

$$=$$

$$twelve\ plus\ one$$

93. Deer Throws

Your task is to make three words from the letters below.

Can you do it?

94. Nine Blank Cards

A sadistic princess is feeling bored and wants to play a game with her 9 servants. She shows them 10 cards: 9 of them are blank, 1 of them has a skull on it. Then, she shuffles them and places them face down. One by one, each servant must flip over a card. The servant who flips over a skull will be beheaded. If it's a blank card, the servant can peek at two of the remaining cards. He then has the option to flip over one of those two cards, both cards, or no cards.

For example, let's say a servant flips over a blank. He then selects two more cards and sees a blank and a skull. Obviously, he would not flip over the skull. He could either flip over the blank card or leave it alone.

The servants are not allowed to talk to each other or make funny gestures during the game.

Feeling generous, the princess tells them the first servant will be spared if he is unlucky enough to flip over a skull card. In that case, she'll just restart the game.

The servants have a few minutes to talk to each other. What is their best strategy?

95. Game Show For Logicians 2

The game show for people with amazing logic skills has grown in popularity. The producers decide to make the game harder to win.

First, three contestants are placed in standing positions. The host then shows them 5 stickers: 3 smiley face stickers, and 2 sad face stickers. One by one, he puts a sticker on each person's back. The host hides the remaining 2 stickers. The result is shown in the diagram below.

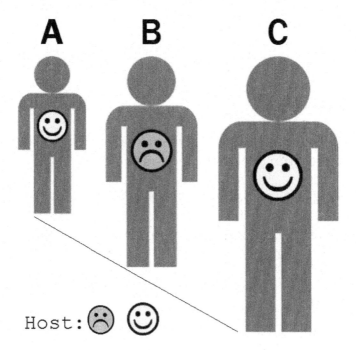

* A's back is facing the other contestants and therefore can't see any of them

* B is facing the same direction as A and can only see A's back. B can't see C at all

* C is also facing the same direction as A and B, and can see both A and B's backs

If any of the contestants can correctly guess the type of sticker on his back, the whole group wins the grand prize. If any of them guesses wrong, they all lose.

Game Show Rules:

* The contestants are not allowed to talk to each other or say anything except to guess their sticker

* The contestants are not allowed to move, turn around, make hand gestures, etc.

The host tells the contestants they have 60 seconds to give an answer, and the game begins. 50 seconds into the game, none of the contestants has provided an answer. Realizing that B and C haven't answered, A believes he knows with a hundred percent certainty the type of sticker on his back. He gives the correct answer, and the whole group wins.

How did contestant A figure out the type of sticker on his back?

96. Golomb Rulers

A standard 12-inch ruler has 13 marks, one for each number from 0 to 12.

A Golomb ruler is something special. It can measure more lengths than there are marks on the ruler. For example, the ruler below only has 4 marks (at 0, 1, 4, and 6), but it can measure any length from 1 to 6. You can measure 5 from 1 to 6. You can measure 3 from 1 to 4. And you can measure 2 from 4 to 6.

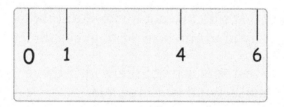

Your job is to create a new 12-inch ruler with the fewest number of marks possible, yet still be able to measure all lengths from 1 to 12.

You'll need a mark at 0 and a mark at 12. What else is required?

97. Hidden Meaning

What's the meaning of the sequence of letters below?

H I J K L M N O

98. Fake Bills Detector

You have a job at the bank sorting out fake bills from real bills. Of course, you can't do this simply by eye. There's a bizarre machine you have to use.

The machine has three slots. Each slot accepts a stack of bills. You can choose to use just one slot, two slots, or all three slots at the same time. When ready, you can press a button on the machine, and the slot or slots that have fake bills will light up. The slot that doesn't light up doesn't have any fake bills.

You need to check a stack of 15 bills. Based on experience and intuition, you know that one of them is fake.

How should you operate the machine so that you can identify the 1 fake bill in the fewest number of checks?

99. Playing With Sticks

On a boring day, you think up a Math game to play by yourself. You have 9 sticks, and you want to see how many correct equations you can make from them.

Game Rules:

* You aren't allowed to break the sticks into smaller sticks

* You can use the sticks to represent Roman numerals and the following Math symbols: addition, subtraction, multiplication, division, and the equal sign.

* You must use all 9 sticks

After a surprisingly long time, you finally come up with one possible solution:

Can you think of at least one more equation?

100. Alien Language Dictionary

You're learning an alien language and need to know the English definition for the following 9 words:

APUNUJA

CRHELNY

DIPPXAVE

ESTUGOR

GWENVEL

HMEBDON

PERAIQUI

TAMBOLOZ

WVALGA

Earthlings have created an electronic dictionary that will take any input from the alien language and provide an output in English. For example, if you feed the dictionary the word 'apunuja,' it will output 'money.' If you feed it three words at a time, such as 'crhelny dippxave estugor,' it will also output three words, such as 'carrot mother dog,' However, the output is always in random order. So, the word 'crhelny' doesn't necessarily mean 'carrot.' Even worse, it takes the dictionary an hour to run a translation, regardless of the number of words you feed it!

You have three hours before your language assignment is due. How can you use the dictionary effectively so that you learn the meaning of the 9 words in time?

Can't get enough?

ACTIVITY BOOKS FOR KIDS
VOLUME #1

The
ULTIMATE
Puzzle
Book

visual exercises
math problems
brain teasers
logic puzzles
word games
mazes

$E = MC^2$

J.J. WIGGINS

Grab this huge activity book packed with mazes,
riddles, word games, and much more!

Hours of fun guaranteed.

Answers

1. Message From Afar

The aliens are friendly. Their message says, "PEACE" (read top to bottom).

2. On Valentine's Day

The phone number is: 214-314-1984.

Valentine's Day is on February 14, which is 214.

Pie is a Math term commonly represented as three digits: 3.14.

George Orwell wrote a book called 1984.

3. John's Car

Molly is the name of the car.

4. Making Muffins

Here are the steps to get a quarter cup of sugar into the batter:

* Fill the 2/3 cup with sugar
* Pour the sugar from the 2/3 cup into the 1/2 cup until the 1/2 cup is full. This leaves you with 1/6 of a cup of sugar in the 2/3 cup (Simple fractions: 2/3 - 1/2 = 1/6)
* pour the 1/6 of a cup of sugar into the batter
* empty the 1/2 cup back into the sugar bag
* Repeat the above steps. You have now poured 1/6 of a cup of sugar into the batter TWICE, which gives you exactly 2/6, which is 1/3 of a cup of sugar

5. The Angry Astrologist

The correct code is 1031.

The drawings on the wall represent the zodiacs: a set of scales = Libra, fishes = Pisces, goat = Capricorn. The table shows you which months those signs correspond to.

Libra – September-October or 9-10
Pisces – February-March or 2-3
Capricorn – December-January or 12-1

Since the drawings are from left to right, you have several combinations to work with. The code can be any of the following:

9-2-1
9-2-12
9-3-1
9-3-12
10-2-1
10-2-12
10-3-1
10-3-12

You can eliminate all the non-4-digit codes, leaving you with only four possibilities. The final clue is in the angry astrologist's announcement. She mentions, "my favorite holiday." The only 4-digit code that is a holiday is 10-3-1.

6. Folding Shirts

To understand what went wrong, we'll have to figure out Steve and Melanie's folding speeds.

Melanie can fold 100 shirts in 90 minutes, which is 9/10 minutes per shirt (a little less than a minute).

Steve can fold 90 shirts in 90 minutes, which is 1 minute per shirt.

Since their folding speeds don't change, we can use their speeds to calculate how long they'll take to fold any number of shirts.

Melanie – 105 shirts

Folding Time = Folding Speed x Number of Shirts
Folding Time = 9/10 x 105 = 94.5 minutes

Steve – 95 shirts

Folding Time = Folding Speed x Number of Shirts
Folding Time = 1 x 95 = 95 minutes

As you can see, even with 10 more shirts to fold, Melanie still manages to finish 30 seconds before Steve.

7. Mystery Man

It's Mario!

8. Three-Legged Race

Your team can complete the track in 24 minutes and 45 seconds. Here's how:

* Chris and Martha walk first (10 minutes)
* Chris runs back to the beginning (45 seconds)
* Chris and Jacky walk (7 minutes)
* Jacky runs back to the beginning (1 minute)
* You and Jacky walk (6 minutes)

Total time: 24 minutes and 45 seconds.

9. Lily's Birthday

Guests must bring items that start with the last letter of their name. For example, "Eric" ends in C, so he brings cake.

Sally can bring anything that starts with the letter Y: yogurt, yam, yoyo, etc.

10. Lost Time

Springfield and Louisville are in different time zones. Louisville is 1 hour ahead. After driving for 4 hours, it was 12:00 AM in Springfield, but already 1:00 AM in Louisville. That night while Jack was sleeping, Daylight Saving Time happened, and clocks moved forward by 1 hour. He slept for 8 hours and lost 1 hour, so he woke up at 10:00 AM.

11. Next Tuesday

1 day.

If tomorrow is two days before Tuesday, then tomorrow is Sunday. Then today is Saturday. Two days from today is two days after Saturday, which is Monday. Counting from Monday, the number of days before it's Tuesday is 1.

12. Strange Sentences

D) is the odd one out. It is the only sentence in which the first letters of each word doesn't spell a school subject.

A) Matrices are too hard! (MATH)
B) Maracas, ukuleles, saxophones, Irish castanets. (MUSIC)
C) Human intentions strange; they often remember yesterday. (HISTORY)
D) Stars, planets, asteroids, comets. Endless. (SPACE)
E) So, can I eat now (chewing everything)? (SCIENCE)

13. Lara's Choice

Lara should choose tunnel A. The bunnies are "man"-eating, and she is a woman.

14. A Simple Word Game

"Field" refers to an enclosed area in a letter. For example, the letter A, D, and O have one field, so they are worth 1 point. The letter B has two fields, so it is worth 2 points.

Therefore, WORD GAME is worth 4 points.

15. A Strange Party

None. One of the two people that can shake hands with each other will always be the first to say "hello," or they all remain quiet.

16. Three Different Jobs

Since Mary is afraid of blood, she can't be the nurse. And since she doesn't like kids, she can't be the elementary school teacher. So she must be the police officer.

Steve doesn't like kids, so he can't be the elementary school teacher. And since Mary is the police officer, Steve must then be the nurse.

17. New Math

The "@" operation means three different Math operations: subtraction, addition, and multiplication.

Example:

8@5 = {8-5}{8+5}{8x5} = {3}{13}{40} = 31340.

So 7@6 = {7-6}{7+6}{7x6} = {1}{13}{42} = 11342.

18. Family Day

He's in the basement playing ping pong with Tracy.

19. Milk And Eggs

To solve this, you must know which number key the letters in MILK and EGGS correspond to.

1 = [blank], 2 = ABC, 3 = DEF, 4 = GHI, 5 = JKL, 6 = MNO, 7 = PQRS, 8 = TUV, 9 = WXYZ, 0 = [blank]

So, MILK = 6455, and EGGS = 3447.

"MILK and EGGS" means you add the two numbers.

6455 + 3447 = 9902.

The phone's password is 9902.

20. Two Lies And A Truth

Mindy is the one telling the truth.

Case #1:

Mark is lying, and Mindy confirms this by telling the truth. Mary is also lying and is the smartest of the group.

Mary says, "I'm not." – LIE
Mark says, "Mindy is." – LIE
Mindy says, "Mark is lying." – TRUTH

Case #2:

If Mary is telling the truth, then she's not the smartest. If Mark is lying, then Mindy is also not the smartest. But that means Mindy must be telling the truth (that Mark is lying), and we can only have 1 truth teller.

Mary says, "I'm not." – TRUTH
Mark says, "Mindy is." – LIE
Mindy says, "Mark is lying." – LIE

Case #3:

If Mary is lying, it means she's the smartest. But if Mark is also telling the truth, then Mindy is also the smartest, which is not possible.

Mary says, "I'm not." – LIE
Mark says, "Mindy is." – TRUTH
Mindy says, "Mark is lying." – LIE

21. Mystery Letters

The answer is T. They are the names of the first several letters of the Greek alphabet.

Alpha Beta Gamma Delta Epsilon Zeta Eta Theta

22. Spiders And Dead Flies

The room has 8 corners, so there are 8 spiders.

23. Penguin Escape

There are 3 zookeepers and 3 penguins. Here's the plan to cross the river:

* 2 zookeepers and 1 penguin CROSS the river
* 1 zookeeper RETURNS
* 1 zookeeper and 1 penguin CROSS the river
* 1 zookeeper RETURNS
* 2 zookeepers and 1 penguin CROSS the river

All 3 zookeepers and penguins return to the zoo.

24. Out Of Order

February comes next. The months are listed from least to most number of letters.

25. Two Dancers

The dancers are Nancy's brothers.

26. Cute Little Things

The answer is RATS.

Grab one of these from the night sky

What's in the night sky? Stars. "One of these" would be a STAR.

And flip it around

If you flip STAR around, you get RATS.

27. World Map

Only 1 country separates Poland and North Korea, and it's Russia.

28. Splitting Spaghetti

Ask one kid to split the spaghetti into two bowls and let the second kid choose the bowl he or she wants.

29. Counting Numbers

You must read the numbers in each row aloud, and that becomes the number in the next row. So,

2 – "One two"
12 – "One one, one two"
1112 – "Three ones, one two"
3112 – "One three, two ones, one two"
132112 – "One one, one three, one two, two ones, one two"

The answer is: 1113122112.

30. Three Coins

Tyler has 1 penny, 1 nickel, and 1 dime. "One of them is not a penny or a nickel" means that one of the other two coins could (and must) be a dime. "The other two are not dimes" means that they must be either pennies or nickels.

31. Thirty Apples

It's impossible. After taking 6 apples each for a total of 24 apples, there are 3 apples remaining in the basket, not 1.

32. Death Or Freedom

You should go with option b) switch to the other face-down card. There are two possible cases.

Case #1

The cards are: DEATH, FREEDOM, FREEDOM.

In this case, if a DEATH card is revealed, you can't lose by switching cards, because both remaining cards are FREEDOM.

Case #2

The cards are: DEATH, DEATH, FREEDOM.

In this case, when a DEATH card is revealed, you may still end up with the other DEATH card whether you switch or not. However, there is a greater probability that you will get the FREEDOM card by switching. Why is this?

Suppose you pick Card A without looking at it. There is a 1 in 3 chance that it is FREEDOM. This means that there is a 2 in 3 chance that FREEDOM is under one of the other cards. When a DEATH card is revealed in the group of two cards, the probability that the other card is FREEDOM does not change. There's still a 2 in 3 chance that it is FREEDOM, and your card still has a probability of 1 in 3. It is therefore a better option to switch cards.

33. Counting Heads

There are 12 heads on the bus.

The number of passengers who get on and off even each other out after three stops, leaving the bus with 10 passengers plus Mimi. Including the bus driver, there are 12 heads.

34. Playing With Percentages

It's less than the number you started with. Suppose you started with 100. You decrease it by 50%, leaving you with 50. Then, you increase it by 90%, giving you 95, which is less than 100.

35. Cash And Points

You can collect as many as 19 points.

* You have $154. You spend $150 to get 15 points, leaving you with $4 + $30 cash back = $34
* With $34, you spend $30 to get 3 points, giving you 15 + 3 = 18 points, and leaving you with $4 + $6 cash back = $10
* With $10, you spend $10 to get 1 point, giving you 18 + 1 = 19 points, and leaving you with $2 cash back

36. Twin Brothers

She can ask one of them, "If I asked your brother if his name was 'John,' would he answer 'Yes?'"

John would answer, "Yes" because he knows that his brother, Jake, would say "No."

Jake would answer, "No" because he knows that his brother would lie about not being named "John."

She could also ask, "If I asked your brother if his name was 'Jake,' would he answer 'Yes?'"

John would answer, "No" because he knows that his brother, Jake, would say "Yes."

Jake would answer, "Yes" because he knows that his brother would lie about not being named "Jake."

Based on the answer from just one of the twins, the mother can figure out who he is.

37. A Pair Of Jeans

The pair of jeans cost $52.50, and you paid $2.50 in tax.

38. A Fast Foot Race

If you're in first place, the person who overtakes you becomes first, and you fall to second place.

39. Sarah's Mother

Sarah's mother's name is Joanne.

40. Around The World

The art thief is making a trip "around the world."
Each country she visits corresponds to a letter in
that phrase.

Australia

Russia

Oman

Uruguay

New Zealand

Denmark

Thailand

Hungary

The next letter is E. Any country starting with that
letter is correct. Examples: Egypt, Ecuador,
Ethiopia.

41. Rock, Paper, Scissors

32 matches. After every match, there is 1 loser. So
after 32 matches, there are 32 losers, and 1
champion.

42. Three Switches

All of them should be left in NEUTRAL.

Since there are no switches to the left or right of a switch set to NEUTRAL, it means the first and third switches must be set to NEUTRAL.

The middle switch can't be UP or DOWN because then the amount of UP switches and DOWN switches won't be the same. So, the middle switch must be NEUTRAL as well.

43. Vowels And Consonants

One possible answer is:

There are <u>twenty-one</u> vowels and <u>thirty-nine</u> consonants in this sentence.

44. Hidden Animal

The hidden animal is HIPPOPOTAMUS, from the blank letters of each word.

45. Alex's Family

Alex is a girl. Scott has a sister.

46. Who's Playing What

There isn't enough information to know.

It's not definitely true or false, because we can't know whether people playing Roblox and Minecraft are also playing Pokemon Go.

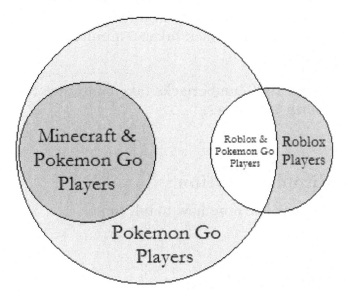

47. Five Golden Rings

You receive golden rings from days 5 to 12, which is 8 days in total.

5 golden rings x 8 days = 40 golden rings.

48. Underwater

Fish breathe oxygen.

49. A Thousand Lumberjacks

If it takes 5 lumberjacks 5 minutes to chop down 5 trees, then 1 lumberjack takes 5 minutes to chop down 1 tree.

Therefore, 1000 lumberjacks take 5 minutes to chop down 1000 trees.

50. Simple Addition

Charlie was learning how to tell time.

51. Birthday Candles

You should buy 6 candles: 9, 9, 0, 0, 1, 1.

52. Cryptic Poem

Each line has two words or phrases that are anagrams of each other.

*An **astronomer** is a **moon starer***
*The **statue of liberty** is **built to stay free***
*To **listen** is to be **silent***
*The **eyes**, they **see***

53. Strange Letter Sequence

HAIRSPRAY.

54. Impossible Age?

I was just born, so I am 0 years old. Mark is 3.

55. Double Money

Sally owed Tom at least $175.

At the beginning of the first month, she pays him $100.

The remainder doubles:
2 x ($175 - $100) = 2 x $75 = $150

The next month, she pays him another $100.

The remainder doubles again:
2 x ($150 - $100) = 2 x $50 = $100

The third month she pays him the remaining $100 an no longer owes him any more money.

Sally could have also owed Tom $350 (or N times $175) and made monthly payments of $200 (or N times a monthly payment of $100).

56. Big Family

Carl, Maggie, Tyler, and Jimmy.

57. Mystery Words

S A N D does not belong. It's the only word in the group that has a common letter with the other 4 words.

The other 4 words do not have any letters in common with each other.

58. Zombie Virus

The virus takes 29 days to infect half the world. On day 30, that number doubles, and the whole world is infected.

59. Kitchen Gloves

20 days.

The right-handed gloves will last for 15 days. On day 16, she can flip the left-handed gloves inside out and use them on her right hand.

Another way to look at it is every 2 days, 3 gloves are used up (the left hand uses 1, and the right hand uses 2).

If Martha uses 3 gloves in 2 days, then she uses 30 gloves in 20 days.

60. It's Thanksgiving Again

Amy's parents are from Canada, where Thanksgiving is celebrated in October.

61. Blind Date

The flight attendant, the nurse, and the receptionist are all men.

62. Mandy's Sister

Mandy is the <u>name</u> of Jessica's sister.

63. Even Heart

You should turn over the 12 and the CLUBS cards.

Since the rule is "if the number is EVEN," we need to verify that the 12 card doesn't have a CLUBS symbol on the back, and we need to verify that the CLUBS card doesn't have an EVEN number on the other side.

We don't need to check the HEART card because it doesn't break the rule whether the other side shows an ODD or EVEN number. This is also true for the 7 card; it doesn't matter whether the other side has a HEART or CLUBS.

64. The Jackson Family

There are 5 people in the Jackson family: Mr. Jackson, Mrs. Jackson, the 2 daughters (who are sisters to each other), and 1 son (the sisters' brother).

65. Red Fruits

The watermelon hasn't been cut, so it's green. The tomato is still raw, so it's green. The apple is green.

66. Body Painting

The artists can finish their body painting job in 3 hours.

* Artist #1 paints the front of Model #1, and Artist #2 paints the front of Model #2 (1 hour)

* Artist #2 paints the back of Model #1, and Artist #2 paints the front of Model #3 (1 hour)

* Artist #2, now done with Model #1, paints the back of Model #2, and Artist #2 paints the back of Model #3 (1 hour)

67. Strange Seating Plan

Here's one possible solution.

Peter	Mark	Francine
Cindy	Patricia	Joseph
Andy	Carol	April

68. Game Show For Logicians

If B and C both had smiley face or sad face stickers, A would've been able to guess his sticker immediately. But since A only sees 1 smiley face sticker and 1 sad face sticker, he can't be certain of the sticker on his back.

B realizes that since A is unsure, he must have a different type of sticker than C. He knows he has a sad face sticker.

69. Two Swimmers

The swimmers are standing on opposite sides of the swimming pool facing each other.

70. Jake's Family

"My mother's son" either refers to Jake or his brother. Since Jake has no children, it's talking about his brother. Jake's brother is the girl's father, so Jake is the girl's uncle.

71. Seven Sevens

Press the keys in the following order:

7 + 7 = ✗ 7 + 7 + 7 + 7 + 7 =

72. Escape The Tombs

This is how fast Luke and Adam can explore the tunnels.

	Tunnel A	Tunnel B	Tunnel C
Luke	1 minute	2 minutes	5 minutes
Adam	3 minutes	6 minutes	15 minutes
Luke & Adam	2 minutes	4 minutes	10 minutes

They spend 10 seconds talking and come up with the following strategy: Adam will wait in the main area while Luke explores two of the three tunnels.

Worst Case Scenario:

* Luke walks to the end of Tunnel B (2 minutes)

* Luke returns to the main area (2 minutes)

* Luke explores Tunnel A (1 minute). He yells back to Adam

* Adam starts walking Tunnel C, and Luke returns to the main area (1 minute)

* Adam keeps walking, and Luke eventually catches up to him in Tunnel C at roughly 1/10 of the way through (about 30 seconds later)

* Luke carries Adam on his back and walks the remaining 9/10 of the Tunnel (9 minutes)

Luke and Adam make it out of the tombs in 15 minutes and 30 seconds.

73. Four Heads Or Tails

No matter which coins are HEADS or TAILS at the beginning of the game, you can always win by following these steps.

* Pick 2 coins that are diagonally opposite of each other and flip them to HEADS

* Pick any 2 coins that are next to each other. At least one will be HEADS from the previous step. If there's a TAILS coin, flip it. If you haven't won yet, it means there are now 3 HEADS coins and 1 TAILS coin

* Pick 2 coins that are diagonally opposite of each other. If there's a TAILS coin, flip that to HEADS and you win. If both are HEADS, flip one of them to TAILS. You now have 2 HEADS and 2 TAILS that are next to each other

* Pick any 2 coins that are next to each other and flip them. If both were HEADS or TAILS, you win. Otherwise, you now have 2 HEADS and 2 tails diagonally opposite of each other

* Pick 2 coins that are diagonally opposite of each other and flip them. You now have 4 HEADS or 4 TAILS

74. The Spy's Secret

The spy is in London, Canada.

The list of possibilities are:

Canada	Paris, London, Vancouver
England	Birmingham, London, Oxford
France	Lyon, Nice, Paris
USA	Paris, Vancouver

Agent #1 says, "...there's no way you can figure out the country." He can only be this confident if the country he received does not have unique city names. If for example Agent #2 received Birmingham, Oxford, Lyon, or Nice, Agent #2 would immediately know the country as well. Knowing this, every city in England and France can be eliminated, leaving Canada and the USA.

Sensing Agent #1's confidence, Agent #2 is then able to deduce the country. How so? The city he received must be unique among Canada and the USA, i.e. London.

When Agent #2 announces he knows, Agent #1 also comes to the same conclusion. The spy is in London, Canada.

75. Cows Beneath Antarctica

Each word in the sentence begins with a letter of the alphabet, starting from Z, all the way to A.

76. Cheese Cutting

You can have as many as 27 pieces.

Make the first cut from top to bottom for 3 pieces. Make the second cut from top to bottom and perpendicular to the first cut, giving you 9 pieces. Then, make the final cut sideways, giving you 27 pieces.

77. Wally's Weight

If Wally's weight is 50 kilograms and half his weight, then his weight is half his weight and half his weight. Therefore, half his weight is 50 kilograms, and so his full weight is 100 kilograms.

78. Letter Pattern

The letter O.

All of the letters can be flipped horizontally and still look the same.

79. Buttons On, Buttons Off

Press the following buttons in any order: A1, C3, A3, C1, B2.

* This is the result after you press buttons A1 and C3

	A	B	C
1	ON	ON	OFF
2	ON	OFF	ON
3	OFF	ON	ON

* This is the result after you press buttons A3 and C1

	A	B	C
1	ON	OFF	ON
2	OFF	OFF	OFF
3	ON	OFF	ON

* Then, pressing button B2 completes the panel

	A	B	C
1	ON	ON	ON
2	ON	ON	ON
3	ON	ON	ON

80. The Numbers Freak

The correct answer is 4. The numbers freak wants you to respond with the number of letters in the number he says.

1 = ONE = 3 letters
2 = TWO = 3 letters
3 = THREE = 5 letters
4 = FOUR = 4 letters
5 = FIVE = 4 letters

81. Kitchen Counter

Cut the 8x5 slab down the middle into two pieces of 4x5 slabs. They can now be reattached to make a 10x4 slab.

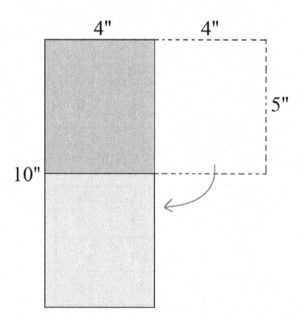

82. Mothers And Daughters

There are two families.

Family #1: Daughter, mother, mother's mother (2 mothers and 2 daughters)

Family #2: Daughter, mother (1 mother and 1 daughter)

83. Spies And Traitors

Yes, a secret agent is spying on a traitor. Joseph's role determines this. If Joseph was a secret agent and he is spying on Cindy, a traitor, the statement is true. If Joseph was a traitor, then Tom, a secret agent, is spying on a traitor, which also makes the statement true.

84. Three Brothers

So, Marty is also older than Jimmy.

85. Fast And Furious

I'm a RACECAR.

86. The Camping Trip

Tamara brought eggs and a tent.

To solve this, we'll draw a grid to keep track of who's bringing what.

* Marty brought steak: We mark this with a Y. Marty doesn't bring other food, and no one else brings steak

	tent	tarp	canoe	steak	eggs	potatoes
Josephine				N		
Marty				Y	N	N
Tamara				N		
steak						
eggs						
potatoes						

* The person with the tent brought eggs: We mark Y where tent and eggs intersect

	tent	tarp	canoe	steak	eggs	potatoes
Josephine				N		
Marty				Y	N	N
Tamara				N		
steak	N					
eggs	Y	N	N			
potatoes	N					

90

* Josephine either owns the canoe or she brought potatoes, and not both: We mark an N for where canoe and potatoes intersect

	tent	tarp	canoe	steak	eggs	potatoes
Josephine				N		
Marty				Y	N	N
Tamara				N		
steak	N					
eggs	Y	N	N			
potatoes	N		N			

We now know that the person who owns the canoe also brought steak, and that person is Marty.

Since Marty owns the canoe, Josephine must've brought potatoes.

Which means Tamara brought the eggs and tent.

Josephine also brought the tarp.

	tent	tarp	canoe	steak	eggs	potatoes
Josephine	N	Y	N	N	N	Y
Marty	N	N	Y	Y	N	N
Tamara	Y	N	N	N	Y	N
steak	N	N	Y			
eggs	Y	N	N			
potatoes	N	Y	N			

87. Two Elevators

This should be their plan:

* 7 people get on Elevator B and head to floor 11 (30 seconds)

* 7 people get off Elevator B and 6 ride Elevator A down to the ground floor, while 1 person stays behind on floor 11, and Elevator B is called up to floor 21 by the remaining 13 people (30 seconds)

* The person who stayed behind calls Elevator A to floor 11, while 7 more people ride Elevator B down to floor 11 (30 seconds)

* 7 people get off Elevator B and ride Elevator A down to the ground floor, while 1 person stays behind, and Elevator B is called up to floor 21 by the remaining 6 people (30 seconds)

* The person who stayed behind calls Elevator A to floor 11, while the last 6 people ride Elevator B down to floor 11 (30 seconds)

* The person who stayed behind joins the 6 people, and they all ride Elevator A down to the ground floor (30 seconds)

The total time comes to 3 minutes.

88. They Come In Pairs

Jessica has 5 pieces of clothing (2 socks, 2 gloves, and a pair of jeans).

89. Pokemon Average

The ten friends talk and agree on the following method:

The counting will begin with Dan. He adds a secret number that only he knows to the number of pokemon he's captured. It can be any number. Let's say this secret number is 100.

So, 151 + 100 = 251.

He tells the next person (Steve) this number. Steve then adds his pokemon captured to this number.

So, 251 + 223 = 474.

He tells the next person this number, and so on.

The process continues until the last person (Natalie) has added her pokemon captured.

The total is 1390. Natalia tells this number to Dan.

Dan subtracts his secret number from the total, giving him 1290. He then divides it by the number of people in the group to get the average.

1290 / 10 = 129.

90. The King's Revenge

You should trade with the king.

The are only two possible scenarios based on what you can see.

Scenario #1:

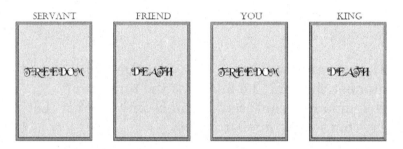

In the scenario, your friend would've trade cards with you and not the servant? Why? Because he knows that you can see the servant's card. On your term, you could simply trade with the servant. Since he traded with the servant, you know it must be the second scenario.

Scenario #2:

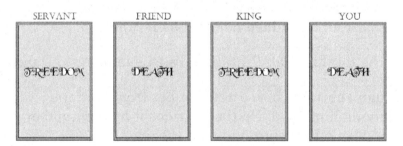

Therefore, you should trade with the king.

91. Unmarried Men

No, we can't be certain. Regardless of how big the family is, all of the men could be married, leaving Cindy (female) to be the adult that's unmarried.

"All of them except two are adults" means there are 2 non-adults (Alice and another child).

"All of them except three are married" means there are 3 unmarried (Alice and 2 other children).

"All of them except four are female" means there are 4 males in the family (father and 3 other children).

The smallest family size that satisfies all of the conditions is 7.

Family Members	
Father	Male
Mother	Female
Cindy	Female
Child #2	Male
Child #3	Male
Child #4	Male
Alice	Female

Alice and Child #4 are the youngest, the rest are adults. In this scenario, both Child #2 and #3 could be the ones that are married.

92. Word Math

If you rearrange the letters in "eleven plus two," you can spell "twelve plus one."

93. Deer Throws

You can make three words by rearranging DEER THROWS into THREE WORDS.

94. Nine Blank Cards

We can assume the first servant will always flip over a blank card. To ensure the other servants don't pick the skull card, he must communicate information to them. They can use the following rules:

* If they peek and see two blank cards, they do not flip any of them over. The next servant will know that both the cards are safe to turn over. He can then turn over one of them and then peek at another two cards

* If they peek and see one blank card and one skull card, they turn over the blank card. The rest of the servants will know not to touch the card left unturned

95. Game Show For Logicians 2

If A and B both had sad face stickers, C would've been able to guess his sticker. But since C sees 1 smiley face sticker and 1 sad face sticker, he can't be certain of the sticker on his back.

If A had a sad face sticker, B would've been able to figure out his own sticker when C remained quiet. But since B sees a smiley face sticker, he can't be certain of the sticker on his back.

A realizes that since B and C are unsure, he must then have a smiley face sticker.

Aside from what's shown in the diagram, there are other combinations of smiley face and sad face stickers, but A can always deduce that his sticker is a smiley face if neither A nor B answers.

96. Golomb Rulers

Here's one possible answer. Did you find another?

97. Hidden Meaning

The sequence letters is "H to O," or H_2O, which is science term for water.

98. Fake Bills Detector

You can identify the fake bill with just 2 checks.

Check #1:

* Split the stack of 15 into four smaller stacks of: 4 bills, 4 bills, 4 bills, and 3 bills
* Insert the stacks of 4 bills into each slot, and set the stack of 3 bills aside
* If none of the slots light up, you know the fake bill is in the stack of 3 bills. Otherwise, one of the slots will light up

Check #2:

* From the fake stack, insert 1 bill into each slot, and set aside the 1 remaining bill (if any)
* If none of the slots light up, you know the fake bill is the 1 bill not in the slots. Otherwise, one of the slots will light up, and that is the fake bill

99. Playing With Sticks

Here are two more possible solutions:

100. Alien Language Dictionary

You have three hours, which means you can only use the dictionary 3 times. Here's how you do it:

INPUT #1	APUNUJA CRHELNY DIPPXAVE ESTUGOR ESTUGOR
OUTPUT #1	CARROT CARROT MONEY DOG MOTHER

* You learn that 'estugor' means 'carrot' since you used it twice

INPUT #2	APUNUJA GWENVEL HMEBDON PERAIQUI PERAIQUI
OUTPUT #2	BIRD MONEY GHOST GHOST SONG

* You learn that 'peraiqui' means 'ghost' since you used it twice
* You learn that 'apunuja' means 'money' since it's the only word you entered for Input #1 and Input #2

INPUT #3	CRHELNY GWENVEL TAMBOLOZ WVALGA WVALGA
OUTPUT #3	FIRE FIRE MOTHER BIRD CHURCH

* You learn that 'wvalga' means 'fire' since you used it twice
* You learn that 'crhelny' means 'mother' since it's the only word you entered for Input #1 and Input #3
* You learn that 'gwenvel' means 'bird' since it's the only word you entered for Input #2 and Input #3
* You learn that 'tamboloz' means 'church' since it's the only other word you didn't know in Input #3
* You learn that 'hmebdon' means 'song' since it's the only other word you didn't know in Input #2
* You learn that 'dippxave' means 'dog' since it's the only other word you didn't know in Input #1

Other Books

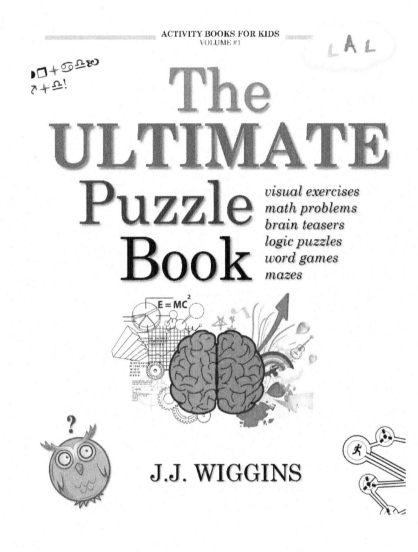

ACTIVITY BOOKS FOR KIDS
VOLUME #1

The ULTIMATE Puzzle Book

visual exercises
math problems
brain teasers
logic puzzles
word games
mazes

$E = MC^2$

J.J. WIGGINS

Want something a little lighter?
Check out these timeless gems!

About The Author

J.J. Wiggins worked in the IT industry where he enjoyed a long and fruitful, yet tedious career. He has since retired and now spends his days with his family, doing his darndest to make them laugh.

http://amazon.com/author/jjwiggins

CPSIA information can be obtained
at www.ICGtesting.com
Printed in the USA
LVOW13s0852040218
565242LV00010B/597/P